P9-CMA-215

Oak Trees

by Kristin Cashore
illustrated by Donna Catanese

PEARSON

Scott
Foresman

Editorial Offices: Glenview, Illinois • Parsippany, New Jersey • New York, New York
Sales Offices: Needham, Massachusetts • Duluth, Georgia • Glenview, Illinois
Coppell, Texas • Ontario, California • Mesa, Arizona

Every effort has been made to secure permission and provide appropriate credit for photographic material. The publisher deeply regrets any omission and pledges to correct errors called to its attention in subsequent editions.

Unless otherwise acknowledged, all photographs are the property of Scott Foresman, a division of Pearson Education.

Photo locators denoted as follows: Top (T), Center (C), Bottom (B), Left (L), Right (R), Background (Bkgd)

Cover ©Lee Snider/Photo Images/CORBIS; 1 ©Roger Wilmshurst; Frank Lane Picture Agency/CORBIS; 7 ©Lee Snider/Photo Images/CORBIS; 8 ©Carl & Ann Purcell/CORBIS; 9 ©Richard Hutchings/CORBIS; 10 ©Roger Wilmshurst; Frank Lane Picture Agency/CORBIS; 11 ©Massimo Listri/CORBIS; 12 ©Philip Gould/CORBIS

ISBN: 0-328-13221-7

Copyright © Pearson Education, Inc.

All Rights Reserved. Printed in the United States of America. This publication is protected by Copyright, and permission should be obtained from the publisher prior to any prohibited reproduction, storage in a retrieval system, or transmission in any form by any means, electronic, mechanical, photocopying, recording, or likewise. For information regarding permission(s), write to: Permissions Department, Scott Foresman, 1900 East Lake Avenue, Glenview, Illinois 60025.

5 6 7 8 9 10 V010 14 13 12 11 10 09 08 07

leaves

branches

trunk

bark

This is an oak tree. Have you ever seen one?

An oak tree has gray or black bark. Its trunk is large. An oak tree has thin branches and green leaves in spring and summer. Oak trees are among the tallest trees around.

How does an oak tree begin its life? An oak tree starts as an acorn. An acorn is a nut with a seed inside. When the seed is planted in the ground, the oak tree starts to grow.

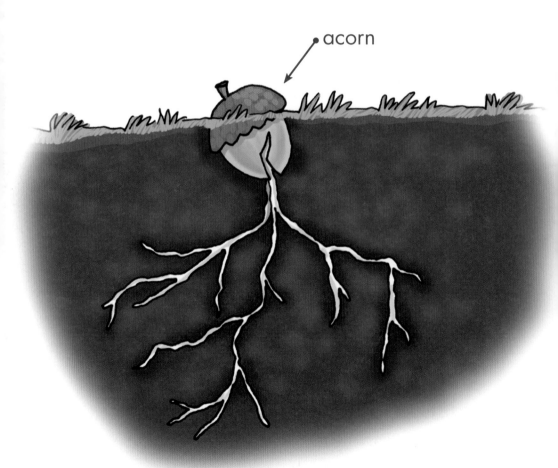

acorn

Oak trees start out small. But then they keep growing and growing!

Water from the soil and light from the sun help the acorn to sprout and grow. Soon another oak tree stretches to the sky.

5

Oak trees can live for hundreds of years. How old do you think this tree is now?

An oak tree reaches high into the air. Some oak trees are more than one hundred feet tall!

One oak tree in Maryland grew to be ninety-six feet tall. Its trunk was thirty-two feet around! It would fill up your bedroom. That tree lived to be 460 years old. Then in 2002, it fell down in a big storm.

This oak tree in Maryland lived 460 years.

There are many large oak trees. It is hard to say which tree is the tallest. It is also hard to say which tree is the oldest. None of these trees live forever. But some live for a very long time!

This oak tree in Virginia is five hundred years old!

In the fall, oak leaves turn many beautiful colors. Then the oak trees drop their leaves.

Have you ever raked leaves in the fall? You could look for oak leaves when you are raking!

An oak leaf looks like this.

Oak trees are home to many animals. Birds like to make nests in oak trees. Squirrels live in oak trees too.

Other animals, instead of living there, use oak trees for food. Deer, bears, and squirrels all eat acorns from oak trees.

This owl made a home for her family in an oak tree.

People also like oak trees. Oak trees give shade from the sun, and they are beautiful to look at.

Wood from an oak tree is good for making chairs and other furniture.

This chair is made of oak wood.

The next time you are out walking, look for an oak tree.

If you like oak trees, you could try planting and growing one of your own. All you need is one acorn!